# JUJUTSU

MASTERING
Martial Arts

# Mastering the Martial Arts Series

**Judo:** Winning Ways

**Jujutsu:** Winning Ways

**Karate:** Winning Ways

**Kickboxing:** Winning Ways

**Kung Fu:** Winning Ways

**Martial Arts for Athletic Conditioning:** Winning Ways

**Martial Arts for Children:** Winning Ways

**Martial Arts for Women:** Winning Ways

**Ninjutsu:** Winning Ways

**Taekwondo:** Winning Ways

# JUJUTSU

## NATHAN JOHNSON

**Series Consultant**
**Adam James**
10th Level Instructor
Founder: Rainbow Warrior Martial Arts
Director: Natl. College of Exercise Professionals

**MASON CREST**
www.masoncrest.com

**Mason Crest Publishers Inc.**
**450 Parkway Drive, Suite D**
**Broomall, PA 19008**
www.masoncrest.com

Copyright © 2015 Mason Crest, an imprint of National Highlights Inc.

Library of Congress Cataloging-in-Publication Data on file at the Library of Congress and with the publisher

Series ISBN: 978-1-4222-3235-4
Hardback ISBN: 978-1-4222-3237-8
EBook ISBN: 978-1-4222-8665-4

First Edition: September 2005

Produced in association with Shoreline Publishing Group LLC

Printed and bound in the United States

---

**IMPORTANT NOTICE**
The techniques and information described in this publication are for use in dire circumstances only where the safety of the individual is at risk. Accordingly, the publisher copyright owner cannot accept any responsibility for any prosecution or proceedings brought or instituted against any person or body as a result of the use or misuse of the techniques and information within.

---

**Picture Credits**
Paul Clifton: 6, 8, 11, 17,27, 32, 35, 48, 49, 53.
Dreamstime.com: Belinka 40.
Mary Evans Picture Library: 12, 54,81.
Nathan Johnson: 14, 18, 37, 41, 43, 50 , 59,66,70, 74, 88.
Topham: 55.
Bob Willingham: 24, 38, 56,65, 72.

Front cover image: Stace Sanchez/Kickpics

# CONTENTS

**Words to Understand:** These words with their easy-to-understand definitions will increase the reader's understanding of the text, while building vocabulary skills.

**Sidebars:** This boxed material within the main text allows readers to build knowledge, gain insights, explore possibilities, and broaden their perspectives by weaving together additional information to provide realistic and holistic perspectives.

Jujutsu means "soft technique" or "gentle way."
However, it could be argued that there is very
little that is gentle in jujutsu.

# INTRODUCTION

**The journey of a thousand miles begins with a single step,** and the journey of a martial artist begins with a single thought—the decision to learn and train. The Martial Arts involve mental and emotional development, not just physical training, and therefore you can start your journey by reading and studying books. At the very beginning, you must decide which Martial Art is right for you, and reading these books will give you a full perspective and open this world up to you. If you are already a martial artist, books can elevate your training to new levels by revealing techniques and aspects of history and pioneers that you might not have known about.

The Mastering the Martial Arts series will provide you with insights into the world of the most well-known martial arts along with several unique training categories. It will introduce you to the key pioneers of the martial arts and the leaders of the next generation. Martial Arts have been around for thousands of years in all of the cultures of the world. However, until recently, the techniques, philosophies, and training methods were considered valuable secretes and seldom revealed. With the globalization of the world, we now openly share the information and we are achieving new levels of knowledge and wisdom. I highly recommend these books to begin your journey or to discover new aspects of your own training.

*Be well.*
**Adam James**

**WORDS TO UNDERSTAND**

**aikido** "The way of harmony"; a modern Japanese martial art

**atemi-waza** Nerve-point or pressure-point strikes used in martial arts

**feudal** Describing a social and political system in which peasants work for a powerful landowner in exchange for food and protection

**halberd** A battle-ax and pike mounted on a long handle

**kenpo** General Japanese term for fist art

**nanushi** Agents of brothel keepers during the Edo period in Japan (1603-1867)

**resuscitation** The process of reviving an unconscious person

**yawara-ge** "Peace-making"; fighting without weapons

**yojori-kumi-uchi** Samurai grappling

**yoshin-ryu** "The willow-heart school"; an early version of jujutsu

# What is Jujutsu?

**Jujutsu is a Japanese word that can be translated as "soft technique." This name is also reflected in the later development of another Japanese martial art called judo, meaning "the soft way." While the founder of judo, Dr. Jigaro Kano (1860–1938), is well known, the names of the founders of jujutsu remain shrouded in the mists of time.**

Jujutsu has many different styles, ranging from highly ritualized and ceremonial styles to those that stress modern urban self-defense. Originally, jujutsu seems to have consisted solely of grappling and immobilization techniques, such as seizing and catching, the locking of joints (particularly elbows and wrists), and tripping and throwing techniques. Modern jujutsu has, however, evolved into a more comprehensive art, and now includes the striking of vital points (called **atemi-waza** techniques), blocking and thrusting methods largely drawn from karate and **kenpo** (fist art), and kicking techniques, also drawn from karate.

When choosing a jujutsu school, keep in mind that there are many different ways in which jujutsu schools are organized and run. In fact,

Immobilization techniques form the major part of the instructions for most jujutsu clubs. It is vital to listen for your opponent's submission, which may be verbal, but more ofter then not will occur when he or she "taps out."

some styles of jujutsu vary so widely from others that it can, at times, seem difficult to understand why they are all referred to as jujutsu. Despite the differences, however, most jujutsu schools emphasize respect for the teacher and a discipline that reflects the Japanese origins of the art.

Modern jujutsu has evolved in an attempt to cater to modern (Western) urban needs. It must be borne in mind, however, that modern self-defense requirements place a great strain on ancient systems of unarmed combat, the genesis of which lies in a period before the Industrial Revolution. An example of this is the introduction of guns to Japan during the **feudal** era when, for the first time, a conscripted peasant army was able to defeat an entire army of elite, traditionally trained warriors. Martial arts, such as judo, **aikido,** and jujutsu are often, along with other Japanese martial arts, collectively referred to as budo. The word "budo" is made up of two separate parts: bu, meaning "warrior," and do, meaning "way." Thus, budo means "warrior way."

## THE SAMURAI

The best-known type of warrior in ancient Japan was the samurai. The word "samurai" is often casually used to mean any Japanese warrior, but it originally referred to a warrior who was a member of an elite class. The status of a samurai was rigidly defined and not easy to gain. Anyone could be a bushi (a "fighting man"), but the samurai class was granted only by birth, or by rendering absolutely exceptional combat service in battle. The word "samurai" dates from around the 10th century, although the Japanese military tradition itself actually goes back further than that.

While jujutsu was not a samurai art, the samurai class was supported

**Oriental martial arts like jujutsu generally have codes of chivalry attached to them. Despite the undoubted efficiency of the various martial arts, they are often deeply influenced by profound philosophies such as Zen Buddhism.**

by large numbers of lower-class foot soldiers, who did not get involved in hand-to-hand fighting. Their exploits do not appear in Japanese chronicles of the day, and their successes and failures are not recounted in epic battle literature.

By the 12th century, the samurai were wearing a distinctive type of armor. Samurai armor was made from small iron scales tied together and then lacquered. These scales were joined into armor plates with silk or leather binding cords. This classic armor, which changed little over the centuries, provided a strong, light protection for the body. Its lightness made it possible for the samurai to move quickly and offensively,

This photograph, while convincing, was actually posed for by models during the late 19th century. It shows a group of three samurai warriors carrying a variety of classical Japanese weapons. The principal weapon of the samurai was the curved bladed sword, or katana.

but any judo- or jujutsu-like grappling would only invite a dagger into the ribs or into other such gaps in this light armor.

In the twilight of feudalism, some far-sighted budo-ka (people who practiced budo) realized that, in a fast-changing world, if Japanese "warrior ways" were to survive, they would have to be broadened in scope. This meant that the warrior ways would need to move away from clan loyalty, and become open to commoners and nobles alike. (The samurai still held the right of kirisute-gomen, however, which allowed them to cut down, without question, any member of the lower classes who insulted them.) The arts would have to remain martial in essence, but they would also be used to promote new, socially useful goals, such as discipline, respect for authority, and love of the nation, parents, and emperor. It was in this climate that Japanese jujutsu was born.

## TYPES OF JUJUTSU

There are four basic types of jujutsu. The first type originated with the warrior caste of the Muromachi period (1337–1563), particularly with their tenshin shoden katori shinto ryu tradition. According to Ritsuki Otake, the head teacher of this tradition, this type of jujutsu used a type of grappling called **yawara-ge** (translated as "peacemaking") that could be used, for the most part, without weapons. This statement does not seem wholly correct, however, as certain techniques within this tradition seem to have involved the use of swords. Indeed, it is alleged that Japan's great swordsman, Miyamoto Musashi, studied yawara-ge.

The second type of jujutsu was developed by unarmed laypeople and by experts in civil defense and arrest techniques. One of the funniest (but least noble) uses of this type of jujutsu occurred during the Edo period (1603–1867), when the **nanushi** (the agents of brothel keepers) used it to expel patrons who were drunk or refused to pay.

The third type of jujutsu is the most modern. This type of jujutsu has been developed in countries outside of Japan, where it has been altered, reformed, or otherwise changed to fulfill the requirements of its practitioners. An example of this type is the Brazilian jujutsu of the Gracie brothers. Gracie jujutsu sprang to prominence during the 1990s due to its incredible efficiency and the success rate it achieved in various contests in

## BRAZILIAN JIU-JITSU

 The modern martial art and combat sport of Brazilian Jiu-jitsu was developed from traditional jujutsu and judo in Brazil. Founders Carlos Gracie and Luiz Franca learned judo from several Japanese nationals who settled in Brazil in the early 1900s. They studied under Mitsuyo Maeda, a judo champion in Japan chosen by judo founder Jigoro Kano to help spread the art around the world.

Eventually, Gracie and his family developed their own version of Jiu-jitsu, and issued an open challenge throughout Brazil in grappling and no-holds-barred competitions. Under the leadership of Helio Gracie, Carlos's brother, who was not as big and strong as his opponent, the sport focused on modifying Maeda's techniques to make them more effective for a smaller fighter by using leverage and precision.

Helio Gracie's son Rorion co-founded the Ultimate Fighting Championship (UFC). During the early years of UFC, the fighters often had skills in only one aspect of martial arts, and the grappling skills of Brazilian Jiu-jitsu consistently led to victory. Today, Mixed Martial Arts has developed a well-rounded fighting strategy that includes multiple disciplines; however, Brazilian Jiu-jitsu and grappling are considered a key foundation skill set for the sport. In addition, Brazilian Jiu-jitsu and grappling have become successful combat sports with numerous national and international competitions.

the U.S., Japan, and other countries. These controversial and violent spectacles are perhaps more of a reminder of gladiatorial contests in ancient Rome than a traditional and noble martial art. One thing is certain, however: Gracie jujutsu pushed the name of jujutsu to the top of the list of prominent martial arts.

Perhaps the best-known jujutsu style is **yoshin-ryu** (willow-heart school). The founder of yoshin-ryu was Akiyama Shirobei Yoshitoki, a physician from Nagasaki, Japan, who went to China to study. There, he learned three techniques and 28 different means of **resuscitation** from a man named Pao-Chuan. After this, Yoshitoki decided to further improve his art, and retired to the Temmangu Temple at Tsukushi for 100 days, where he increased the number of techniques in his repertoire to 103.

Yoshin-ryu is named for the supple branches of the willow tree, which Yoshitoki noticed bend and discharge snow as fast as it accumulates. In this way, willow trees escape the fate of hardier trees that get crushed under the weight of the snow.

# A BIT OF HISTORY

Jujutsu developed during the Edo period in Japan in the mid-16th century. People had more leisure time during this period because of a lull in the constant civil war that had occupied Japan over many years.

It is commonly believed that jujutsu was developed on the battlefields of Japan, but this is a misconception. Historically, samurai "grappling" (known as **yojori-kumi-uchi**) involved armed combat, as classical martial artist and scholar Don F. Draeger reveals. According to Draeger, no classical system of bu-jutsu (warrior technique) required a warrior to be unarmed.

It is unlikely that the samurai knew jujutsu. Samurai close-quarters methods of combat involved a short, armor-piercing weapon. According to the noted martial arts historian Steven Turnbull, there is only one well-documented incident concerning the battlefield use of anything even remotely resembling jujutsu. This account was recorded because it was so unusual.

The incident occurred during the Battle of Shizugatake in 1583. It seems to have been started by the reckless act of a wakamusha (a young rearguard warrior) named Kiyomasa. Kiyomasa confronted an experienced opposition general, and both reportedly abandoned their spears. "...It was a combat that has often been depicted in art, showing the young Kiyomasa and the other samurai (whose name is unknown) locked in a rather graceless struggle, very far removed from the ideals of aikido...The two samurai fell off the edge of a cliff and Kiyomasa cut off the older man's head."

Most original jujutsu schools always assumed that fighters were armed—at least with a dagger. Indeed, the range of weapons available to the classical warrior was staggering. A classical warrior's principal weaponry included a long sword, a short sword, a dagger, a spear, a **halberd** (a battle ax and pike mounted on a handle), and a bow and arrows. The list of weapons was always growing, and included everything from innocent-looking iron-framed folding fans to huge, unwieldy muskets. Other examples of weaponry included chain weapons, such as a sickle attached to a weighted chain, and a wooden staff with a small ball and chain at one end. Japanese warriors studied and built schools around every conceivable weapon of the time.

The bulk of weaponless arts were created—or, rather, synthesized—in Japan from the mid-16th century onwards. These arts were largely

These swordsmen are from one of the Japanese schools of ninjutsu. The ninja have been popularized by everything ranging from *Teenage Mutant Ninja Turtles* movies to deadly assassins in popular action movies. Ninjutsu uses many grappling techniques that are similar to those of jujutsu.

developed for use by and against commoners, who were forbidden to carry weapons. Perhaps this is why jujutsu holds such an appeal for the modern age, in which most people do not carry weapons.

## GETTING STARTED

The word ju means "soft," and the word jutsu means "technique." Accordingly, the aim of jujutsu is to achieve the maximum effect with the minimum amount of effort, and thus jujutsu is sometimes referred to as "the gentle way." However, it could be argued that there is very

The uniform, or gi, is a loose-fitting thick cotton jacket and pants tied with a cotton or silk belt, or obi.

little that is gentle in jujutsu. Jujutsu strikes vital points, clamps and shuts off blood vessels, and uses choking techniques to render an opponent unconscious.

Despite all of these seemingly harsh techniques, however, with good instruction and in a safe and professional environment, the demanding discipline of jujutsu can be great fun. It is a good way to get fit, to build stamina and self-confidence, and to improve concentration. It also has great value as a means of self-defense, which, according to many instructors, was the sole reason for its creation.

## CLOTHING

Jujutsu students usually wear a white, heavy, cotton uniform called a gi (pronounced gee), and a belt called an obi (pronounced OH-bee) that shows their rank. Most jujutsu schools have a progressive grading system, with the appropriate grade or rank issued after examination. Jujutsu grades closely follow those found in judo and karate: a beginner starts with a white belt and progresses through yellow, orange, green, blue, purple, brown, and black belts. The white belts through the brown belts are referred to as kyu grades. Black belt grades go from 1 to 10, and are called dan grades.

It is important to ensure that your gi fits comfortably for reasons of both safety and practicality. Students should keep their nails clean and short and remove all jewelry, or tape over any that cannot be removed. Long hair should be tied back. Because jujutsu uses throwing techniques, classes are usually conducted using foam-padded mats for safety. In ancient Japan, woven grass mats called tatami were used.

It is important to perform warm-up exercises before beginning to practice jujutsu. The number and type of warm-up exercises will vary among clubs, but there are some exercises that are fundamental to all.

## ETIQUETTE

Jujutsu, like other Japanese martial arts, practices a code of discipline or ritual behavior, which includes a ritual bow called a rei. The bow is performed either standing or kneeling. The standing bow is performed upon entering or leaving the place of practice (called the dojo) and also to a partner before and after training. Students facing a teacher at the beginning and end of the class perform the kneeling bow.

To bow formally, lower yourself onto your left knee, and take hold of your pants with your right hand. Bring your right foot back without bending your back (just in case you should need to respond quickly to

**Proper etiquette in jujutsu starts with learning the formal bow, or rei, which starts with the hands on the folded knees.**

an attack). Bring your right leg back, and sit on both heels, with your feet flat. Place your hands on your thighs, and relax your arms and your shoulders. Make sure that your knees are no wider than two fists apart.

Prior to performing the bow, place your left hand on the floor in front of your body, followed by your right hand. Finally, bring your head down into a bow. This procedure is usually carried out with the students facing the teacher (called the sensei). The sensei and students bow to each other.

Once the class has "bowed in," either the teacher or a senior student will conduct a warm-up session consisting of conditioning and stretching exercises and stamina or strength-building exercises. These

## FORMAL BOW

**STEP 1:** Keeping your back straight, gently lower yourself to the floor in a dignified way.

**STEP 2:** Stretch out your right leg before kneeling. (This transitional posture still allowed a samurai to draw his sword.)

**STEP 3:** Kneeling as shown in this illustration is known as "seiza." It is used as a formal way of sitting throughout Japan.

**STEP 4:** Place the left hand flat on the floor and lower the head; both of these actions are reminiscent of Japanese feudal customs.

**STEP 5:** Complete the bow, maintaining dignity and concentration.

exercises are done to increase and maintain fitness and flexibility and to help prevent injury.

## MANAGING FEAR

Fear is an integral part of human existence; but it is how we manage it that counts. Fear has both a useful function and a useless function: fear that paralyzes us is useless, whereas fear that prompts us into swift and effective action is useful. If you train in jujutsu, you will experience fear, and this is perfectly normal. Fear can have such a power over us that we can even be afraid of being afraid, which, of course, is not particularly productive.

Fears are often based on our recognition of our limitations, particularly those that we have imposed upon ourselves. To overcome our limitations, it is necessary to face them. The key to facing them is to do so gradually. This is precisely what a properly structured training system will help you to do. Training in jujutsu should, therefore, let you acquaint yourself with certain types of fears, and then help you overcome them. Once this has been done, the feeling of accomplishment brings its own reward, and you can progress to a new challenge.

Fear of personal failure is high on the list of obstacles in jujutsu training. However, by training often, you are given repeated opportunities to work through negative emotions and to succeed. In fact, the benefits of training extend beyond jujutsu and can affect all aspects of your life.

Jujutsu, though action- and combat-oriented, can help you learn to conquer and overcome fears through the use of physical and mental training.

**WORDS TO UNDERSTAND**

**peripheral vision** The 180-degree vision possible when the eyes are unfocused

# BREAK-FALLS

**Before students can learn to throw, trip, or even lock each other, they must first learn the art of breaking a fall. Break-falls are referred to as ukemi, which means more than just "to fall." Proper ukemi allows you to flow, tumble, roll, or safely neutralize the consequences of being thrown.**

It is vital to remain relaxed when practicing break-falls. There are several different types of break-falls: the side fall, the back fall, the front fall, the bridge fall, the forward roll, the backward roll, the side roll, and the diving roll.

When practicing break-falls, safety is of the utmost importance. Nobody wants to fall from a great height. Therefore, when students first learn to fall, they do so from a crouching or squatting position, close to the floor.

The art of falling requires the use of several basic principles. First of all, you must remain relaxed at all times. Certain falls require you to slam the mat with your arms to transfer the momentum of the fall fluidly to the ground. To do this properly, your

**Going…going…gone! These experts are using the proper kind of surface to perform this spectacular throw. Any individual suffering this throw against a hard surface would be liable to serious injury or even death.**

arms must be relaxed. You must learn to exhale upon impact with the ground (or just before) to avoid being winded. The idea is to spread the force of a fall evenly across all contact surfaces. If this is done properly, it will minimize discomfort. At a more advanced level, you will be able to break-fall from higher positions and from a variety of throws.

# HOW TO PERFORM BREAK-FALLS

Safety first is a rule that cannot be stressed enough, particularly where break-falls are concerned. If you are going to practice break-falls, you must do so on the proper floor surface and under competent tuition.

## THE SIDE FALL

**STEP 1: Tilt your body forward to give yourself the feeling of loss of balance.**

**STEP 2: Flip over and sideways to roll/fall onto your side/back, slapping the mat with your arm to absorb the force of the impact.**

**STEP 3: Regain your composure after absorbing the impact of the fall.**

Jujutsu throws are dangerous. You can tell by the vulnerable position of the person being thrown. It is important to remember that jujutsu is no longer used in life-or-death situations. Great trust is needed from both the thrower and the thrown to practice techniques like this.

## JUJUTSU

### THE BACK FALL

You are advised to try this break-fall on a gymnastics "crash mat" for the first few times. Pay particular attention to controlling your head, which, for obvious reasons, must not hit the floor.

## THE SIDE FALL

Step forward onto your right foot, and then throw your left arm and leg upward and to the rear. These actions will create enough momentum to disrupt your center of gravity, making a side fall necessary. Tuck in your head and shoulders toward your waist, spring off your right leg, and tumble over your center points (about waist height), to land on your right side (this is actually called a twisting side fall).

## THE BACK FALL

Bend your knees, and drop your body to a squatting position. Pivot your body to the rear to disrupt your center of gravity at waist height, and throw yourself backward. The landing surface, in this case, your upper back, should touch the ground where your feet were. Make sure you tuck your chin in and breathe out before impact.

## THE FRONT FALL

Flex your knees, and leap up, literally throwing yourself out from underneath your own stance. Your body should momentarily become parallel with the floor and your head should be turned to the side to prevent

## THE FRONT FALL

**STEP 1: Adopt a relaxed stance from which to spring up.**

**STEP 2: Get your body position parallel with the floor.**

**STEP 3: Let your forearms and thighs take the weight of impact upon landing.**

## THE DIVING ROLL

STEP 1: From a running start, reach forward and launch yourself off the ground. Aim to place your body parallel with the ground.

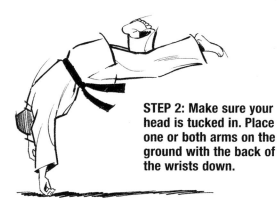

STEP 2: Make sure your head is tucked in. Place one or both arms on the ground with the back of the wrists down.

STEP 3: Tumbling over, as if performing a gymnastic forward roll, complete the diving roll by regaining a balanced upright stance.

your face from hitting the mat. The impact surface should be your forearms and the lower front part of your thighs, and your back should be slightly arched so that your abdomen does not strike the mat.

## THE DIVING ROLL

Although it is undoubtedly an integral part of modern jujutsu, the diving roll is not necessarily used under practical combat conditions and is most commonly seen in demonstrations and exhibitions. It can, however, be used to dive away from an opponent in the most desperate of circumstances.

## UPSETTING BALANCE

Because jujutsu seeks to achieve maximum effect with minimum effort, it is important that an opponent's own force be used against him or her. This means you must learn to use an opponent's force and momentum to gain advantage for yourself. In jujutsu, this is done by going along with the direction of your opponent's force, blending your own force with it and then rerouting it. This tactic, done successfully, should lead to the dramatic downfall of your opponent.

Jujutsu has a reputation for allowing smaller, weaker people to defend themselves against larger, stronger people. It is well known that jujutsu experts are skilled in using their opponents' force for their own benefit. In jujutsu, force should never be met with force. If such a clash

## THE INWARD-OPENING DOOR

The following example illustrates the concept of using your opponent's force for your own benefit. Imagine that you have your shoulder pressed against a door that opens toward you. Someone is pushing the door to try and get in, and you are preventing him or her from doing so. The person begins to push harder; perhaps he or she is stronger than you are. Calmly, you allow the force to build up until it becomes quite a struggle. Suddenly, you let go of the door and slip off to the side, where the hinges are. As the other person crashes through the vacuum you have created, you then get behind him or her and give him or her a push in the direction he or she is stumbling. As the person struggles to save his or her balance and try reversing direction, you (in tandem with the person's force) push in the direction in which he or she is reversing, so that he or she falls over.

Jujutsu has proved to be extremely effective in modern "arena" fighting. Its "no-holds-barred" attitude to combat, plus the results it has achieved, have increased jujutsu's popularity considerably.

were to take place, then the larger, stronger person would win. While in the natural world, the rule usually is that the biggest and strongest win, with properly applied jujutsu, we can say "the bigger they are, the harder they fall."

# UPSETTING AN OPPONENT'S POSTURE

There are several essential elements to upsetting an opponent's posture. One is to disturb your opponent's balance, or equilibrium. The original Japanese expression for this is kuzusu, which means "to break or loosen." Of course, you should always adopt a safe and balanced position yourself.

There are numerous occasions when throws can be applied successfully against an opponent, but the two most basic situations occur when your opponent is in the midst of placing one foot upon the floor while the other foot is in motion, or even off the ground. When an opponent is placing a foot on the floor, he or she will naturally incline his or her body in that direction. This situation provides you with a good opportunity to successfully throw him or her.

An opponent can be "loosened," broken, or unbalanced in six directions: direct front, direct back, left and right front corner, and left and right back corner. In the direct front position, your opponent will be leaning forward, and his or her weight will be resting on his or her toes. In the direct back position, your opponent's weight will be resting backward, on his or her heels. In the left front corner position, your opponent's weight will be inclined to the left, with the toes of his or her left foot facing forward. In the right front corner position, your opponent will be leaning to the right, with the toes of his or her right foot facing forward. In the left back corner position, your opponent will be leaning back and to the left, with his or her left heel behind him or her. Finally, in the right back corner position, your opponent will be leaning back and to the right, with his or her right heel behind him or her.

The technique in which you try to disrupt your opponent's balance, or posture, is called tsuri-komi. Tsuri-komi refers to a pull and a lift upward and toward yourself.

## DISTANCE

There exists within the Japanese martial arts a concept that refers to distance. This concept is called maai. Maai is defined as the relative distance between you and your opponent. The natural distance between yourself and your opponent is approximately the length of your leg. If you ever find an opponent inside this distance, you should already be engaging him or her by controlling his or her limbs, or striking, blocking, throwing, or locking him or her. It might also be necessary to retreat and maintain your maai.

There are two types of natural reflexes that are closely bound up with distance: visual reflexes and touch, or contact, reflexes. Visual reflexes require a lengthy thought process. This is because first you must see (an attack, for example), then you must think about or process what is happening, and then you must respond. Touch, or contact, reflexes, however, are faster than visual reflexes because they bypass the thinking process. Contact reflexes allow the jujutsu practitioner to respond instantly to a situation.

All actions happening outside of your maai will require the use of visual reflexes. All actions happening inside of your maai will require the use of contact reflexes. Visual reflexes are virtually useless inside your natural distance, because the eyes and brain cannot process them quickly enough to be of use to you.

Keeping your own base of support strong even while attacking or defending will help you remain ready for whatever might be coming.

## WHERE TO LOOK WHEN ENGAGING AN OPPONENT

It is said that the eyes are the mirrors of the soul. Eye contact can be provocative. Never assume that you can scare or intimidate someone merely by staring into his or her eyes, particularly if they are inside your natural range. Again, if an opponent is inside your natural range, then you should either be engaging him or her or retreating.

## THE RANGE OF YOUR PERIPHERAL VISION

Human vision extends over a nearly 180-degree arc. Here is an experiment you may care to try in order to better understand this concept. You will need three friends to help you. Stand with one friend to your left, one friend to your right, and one friend directly in front of you. Make sure that they are at least three to five paces away from you. Have one of your three friends raise a hand. You will easily be able to identify who has raised their hand anywhere along the natural 180-degree arc because that is your natural range of peripheral vision.

During an attack, you should pay attention to your **peripheral vision**. Rather than staring at one small part of your opponent, or at the center of his or her body, your sight should be fixed at the edges of your opponent's body. Otherwise, you could miss seeing an attack. By expanding your field of vision, you can take in your opponent's entire body and monitor his or her movements efficiently.

Distracting an opponent and fooling him or her into making a wrong move is a well known technique in many martial arts and is known as a feint—for instance, pretending you are going to throw a high punch but really throwing a low punch. Feinting is easy to understand on a visual (kick, punch) level, but more difficult to carry out successfully in grappling and holding situations. This is because grappling is based on touch or feel, not vision, and it is harder to fool your opponent in such situations. Of course, a martial art like jujutsu would use a combination of visual and touch reflexes.

Sweat, hard work, and sometimes, even pain are all aspects of martial arts like jujutsu, but as the Chinese say: "Those who pick the roses feel the thorns."

## WORDS TO UNDERSTAND

**chi** Chinese term for internal energies
**chudan** Middle level
**gedan** Lower level
**jodan** Upper level
**ki** Internal energy
**meridians** Invisible channels along which chi flows in a human body
**shihonzuki** Four-finger strike

# STRIKING TECHNIQUES

Martial artists are renowned for being able to defend themselves using nothing more than their bare hands. This means that they must learn to transform fists, open hands, elbows, knees, and feet into a range of practical, natural weapons.

## THE FIST SWORD (SEIKEN)

The clenching of the fist is carried out in three steps. First, fold the middle joints of the fingers; next, fold the hand at the base joints of the fingers; last, place the thumb so that its inner edge tightly grips the first two fingers. The front surface of the fist should be as flat as possible. Contact is usually made with the first and second knuckles. This type of regular fist is called a fist sword, also known as a seiken. Although this type of fist may be difficult to make at first, it will become easier with practice.

## ONE-FINGER FIST (IPPON-KEN)

There are two forms of the one-finger fist. The first uses the index finger to strike with, and the second uses the middle finger to strike with.

Kicking techniques like this back-turning kick have been imported from modern karate. A kick like this is capable of breaking wood, tiles, and certainly ribs.

**Martial arts masters from many disciplines stress the importance of correctly forming the fists. One master claimed that it took three years to do it properly.**

To make this fist, protrude the index or middle knuckle from the fist, and hold thethumb firmly against the protruding knuckle.

## IRON-HAMMER FIST (TETSUI)

Clench the fist as in the regular fist sword (see previous section), and use the base of the fist (the edge of the little finger) to make contact.

## SPEAR HAND (NUKITE)

There are three ways of forming the fingers into a spear hand, but the four-finger thrust (known as **shihonzuki**) is the most common. Hold the four fingers tightly together, and press your bent thumb tightly against them. The fingers should be slightly bent, giving the backs of the hand and fingers a slightly ridged appearance.

## TWO FINGER SPEAR HAND THRUST (NIHONZUKI)

Close both the ring finger and the little finger, and bend the thumb so that it lies on top of the ring finger. The two extended fingers are the only points of contact used.

## ONE FINGER SPEAR HAND THRUST (IPPONZUKI)

The one-finger spear hand thrust is similar to the four-finger thrust (see previous section), except that only the index finger is extended.

Some martial arts teachers claim that the fingertips and the edges of the hands are superior to the fist as a weapon. In some jujutsu styles, the fingertips are used against vital points of the opponent's body.

## TOUGHENING THE HANDS

Some styles of jujutsu toughen the hands, feet, or other body weapons by thrusting them into containers full of rice, beans, sand, or pebbles. This practice, however, is strongly discouraged. Skill in the delivery of a particular technique is far more important than the unwanted side effect of developing ugly calluses on your hands.

## THE ELBOW (EMPI)

The elbow point and the flat of the elbow are used at close quarters to strike upward, downward, backward, and horizontally.

## THE KNEE (HIZA)

The knee point is used to strike upward and in a semicircular arc, and also to pin and trap limbs during groundwork, in which combat continues on the ground.

## THE FOOT

Foot techniques significantly expand the arsenal of natural weapons found in Oriental martial arts. Natural weapons on the foot include the toe tips, ball of the foot, top of the arch, little toe, edge of the foot, and heel.

## ATEMI-WAZA

Although they are not strictly classified, jujutsu employs a considerable number of striking techniques, traditionally called atemi-waza.

These strikes include one-, two-, and four-finger strikes; single-knuckle strikes; palm-heel strikes; edge-of-hand strikes; elbow and knee strikes; and some kicks. The advantage of atemi-waza is that it is subtle and requires little power. On the other hand, it requires excellent timing and precise targeting. Moreover, if you get it wrong, you may be vulnerable to a counterattack.

Atemi-waza strikes differ from typical martial arts strikes. They include strikes designed to cause a distraction prior to throwing an opponent, as well as strikes that are designed to cause severe pain, trauma, or even lead to unconsciousness. Not surprisingly, atemi-waza-style strikes are

**Despite the dramatic appeal of kicking techniques, there are fewer instances in which they could be safely used than the movies would have us believe.**

forbidden in all jujutsu sporting competitions because they are considered dangerous. Some examples of atemi-waza are as follows.

# CHOKE ESCAPE

Your opponent grabs you around the throat and tries to strangle you. Turning sideways, and taking care to keep your back straight, bend your knees, and lower your posture. Guard your head with your left hand, and, clenching your right hand into a fist, strike your opponent with the edge of your fist (a hammer-fist blow) to his or her ribs.

## DEFENSE FROM A REAR CHOKE HOLD

**STEP 1: An assailant grabs your neck from behind and attempts to choke you.**

**STEP 2: Turn sharply to face the attacker sideways on and strike hard to his ribs as you drop into a strong stance.**

## PALM-HEEL STRIKE

Apply a palm-heel strike to the chin when an opponent grabs you from a front-facing position. Or, alternatively, apply a palm-heel strike to an opponent's nose or ears.

# PALM-HEEL STRIKE

The instant your opponent grabs you, step in and push, press, slap, or hit him or her with the palm of your hand, taking care to keep the elbow of your striking arm down. There are three possible targets: the chin, the nose, and the ear.

## ELBOW AND KNEE STRIKES

**The elbow strike is extremely powerful and can be used to deadly effect at close quarters.**

**The knee strike is also extremely powerful and best used at close quarters.**

# ELBOW AND KNEE STRIKES

The elbow strike is a technique used by many types of martial art, and many schools consider the use of the elbow to be indispensable. The same applies to the knee strike. The reason that both techniques are so useful is that they can be applied when the defender has little room to maneuver.

# FOOT STAMP

Your opponent grabs you in a bear hug or similar move. Taking care to maintain your balance, raise your leg and drive it downward with a powerful stamping action onto the top (arch) of your opponent's foot.

# BLOCKING, PUNCHING, AND KICKING

Modern jujutsu has synthesized techniques from other martial arts, such as karate. Blocking techniques, an indispensable part of karate, can now be found in similar form in jujutsu. Like striking techniques, blocking techniques are classified into three heights: upper (**jodan**), middle (**chudan**), and lower (**gedan**).

# LOWER-LEVEL BLOCK (GEDAN BARAI)

The lower-level block is used to defend against an attack aimed at a low target, such as the stomach. Place the fist of the blocking hand across your body and near

**FOOT STAMP**

From a bear-hug position, make contact with your opponent's shin using the sole of your foot. Slide down his leg and stomp on the arch of his foot.

**Try to induce movement in your opponent to break his concentration and posture.**

to the side of your jaw and ear. Retract the nonblocking hand strongly to the side of your body as you sweep downward and forward with the blocking hand. Finish with the blocking hand six inches (15 cm) above your knee; your fist should be clenched and your palm facing downward. Your body should not lean forward or backward.

## MIDDLE-LEVEL BLOCK (UDE-UKE)

Cock the blocking arm under the triceps of the opposite arm, with your palm facing down. Block strongly outward and in an arc, rotating your fist so that your knuckles are down and your palm is up. Complete the block by returning the nonblocking hand to the side of your body. The blocking hand finishes in a bent-arm position at the height of your shoulder.

## RISING BLOCK (JODAN AGE-UKE)

Prime your arm for the rising block in the same way as for the middle-level block (see previous section), only this time, sweep your arm

Your body will function with full efficiency only if you move it through proper balanced and strong positions.

**Although size and strength are important factors in a jujutsu practitioner, the use of skillful and effective technique can make up for a lack of size and strength in a jujutsu player, as shown here.**

upwards and forwards, rotating it so that it finishes in a position above your forehead, with your arm bent and the back of the blocking hand twisted to face your chest.

## MIDDLE-LEVEL PUNCH (CHUDAN TSUKI)

Cock or prime your punching hand at the side of your body, just above the hip, making sure that your forearm is parallel with the floor. Thrust the punching hand forward, keeping your elbow in and down. Twist your forearm as you deliver the punch. It should land with the back of your hand facing upwards.

## UPPER-LEVEL PUNCH (JODAN TSUKI)

This punch is performed in the same as the middle-level punch, except is executed with a rising action directed toward the opponent's head.

## KICKING TECHNIQUES (KERI-WAZA)

Modern martial arts have refined and developed kicking techniques to a high degree. Today, kicking techniques form part of the training program of many modern jujutsu styles, even though it can be argued that kicking techniques are not actually part of original jujutsu. Techniques include the front kick (mae-geri), the side kick (yoko-geri), and the round kick (mawashi-geri).

## THE FRONT KICK (MAE-GERI)

Raise the knee of your kicking leg so that it is at least parallel with the floor. Make sure that the knee of the supporting, or platform, leg is well bent and that the supporting foot is pointing forward. Thrust the kicking leg out and forward while pushing the ankle forward and pulling the toes back, so that if the kick were to land, it would make contact using the ball of the foot.

## THE SIDE KICK (YOKO-GERI)

Raise the knee of your kicking leg so that it is at least parallel with the floor. Make sure that the knee of the supporting, or platform, leg is well bent and that the supporting foot is pointing sideways. Turn your hips until the thigh of the kicking leg faces the intended target and the lead hip is in a comfortable position. Thrust the kicking leg sideways and out while bending the ankle and pulling the toes back. The point of contact is with the edge of the foot.

## THE ROUND KICK (MAWASHI-GERI)

Raise the knee of your kicking leg so that it is at least parallel with the floor. Make sure that the knee of the supporting, or platform, leg is well bent and that the supporting foot is pointing sideways. Begin to turn the hip of the kicking leg as you "flick" the leg out in a semicircle. The point of contact should be with either the top of the arch or the ball of the foot.

## THE BACK KICK (USHIRO-GERI)

Pivoting on the ball of your front foot, turn your body 180 degrees. Raise the knee of your kicking leg so that it is at least parallel with the floor. Make sure that the knee of the supporting, or platform, leg is well bent and that the supporting foot is pointing directly backward. Thrust the kicking leg out backward, toward the target. The point of contact should be with the heel.

## HEALING

Healing is an integral part of many—if not all—martial arts systems. Most martial arts healing techniques can be traced back to an extensive system of Chinese medicine. In modern jujutsu, we have recourse to first aid and to Western medical services. However, it may occasionally be necessary to massage, manipulate, or otherwise treat a joint or tendon that has been

Jujutsu is full of contradictions. But ways of making things easier can often be found in the techniques and principles we find the most difficult.

lightly injured. The treatment of injuries in jujutsu is drawn from techniques of Oriental medicine, which seeks to treat the outside injury while at the same time balancing the inner energy.

Drawing on the Chinese concept of **chi** (internal energy), the Japanese have developed the concept of **ki** (also meaning internal energy). Ki, like electricity, cannot be seen, heard, smelled, or tasted, but its effects can be felt. According to Oriental medical beliefs, when a person is ill or injured, it is assumed that his or her flow of ki has been disrupted or blocked. Chinese healing techniques aim to restore the natural flow of ki through invisible channels, called **meridians**.

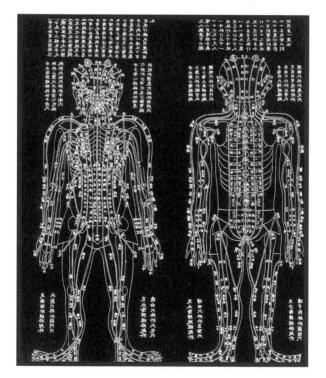

An ancient Chinese acupuncture chart. Traditional Oriental medicine has produced theories, treatments, and practices of staggering complexity.

Extensive use is made of meridians in the popular treatment, acupuncture. In acupuncture, small needles are inserted into the patient's skin at key points along the meridians. Similar to acupuncture is the art of acupressure, which has more to do with jujutsu proper. The Japanese have their own versions of massage and manipulation; one such method is called shiatsu, which has become popular worldwide.

Another Japanese healing art that has also become popular worldwide and that is intimately connected with the theory of ki power is called reiki. Reiki causes healing without the healer ever touching the patient. The patient is healed by a series of special passes and ki-balancing techniques used by the healer.

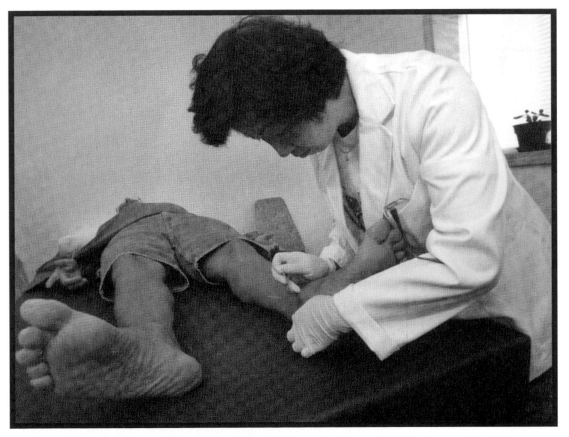

The Japanese people's belief in the existence of energy channels in the human body, known as meridians, is central to their use of methods of acupuncture.

 **WORDS TO UNDERSTAND**

**chi-na** to seize and grapple

**groundwork** actions in a fight performed when both fighters are on the ground

# Joint-Locking and Holding Techniques

**Because jujutsu is generally seen as a means of self-defense, it is more commonly used defensively rather than preemptively. In other words, you often use it to defend yourself from an attack as opposed to instigating one.**

There are two basic approaches to joint-locking and holding techniques. In the first approach, you actively seek to catch, seize, hold, twist, lock, and finally, subdue an opponent. This tactic dates back to jujutsu's predecessor, the ancient Chinese art of **chi-na**, meaning "to seize and grapple." The art of chi-na was used as a means to arrest civilians. Japan inherited this civil-arrest tradition, which it then modified to suit its own national customs.

In the second approach to applying joint-locking and holding techniques, you apply them after having been attacked. The attack may take the form of a strike, punch, kick, or other assault that you must defend against. The attack may also take the form of a restraint applied against you by your opponent. This could be a grip on one or both of your wrists or the seizing of your clothing.

**Taking an opponent to the floor, holding and locking, or immobilizing him or her are the basic goals of jujutsu.**

The following excerpt from the martial arts book *Barefoot Zen* describes the art of chi-na. Here, a martial arts master, Mah Tsu, is chasing a gang of thieves:

"Lok Yui did his best to run despite a smashed leg. The pain was terrible, but not as terrible as the pain that the Triads would inflict on him if they caught him again. With his heart pounding and nausea filling his stomach and fast moving upward, he found someone blocking his path, and he crashed to a halt. The bandit called Locust Eater was in his way.

"A stab of rage rushed through Lok Yui as he recognized the man called Locust Eater, the man who had betrayed him. Looking again, he noticed that Locust Eater's arms were out of sight, which made him look strange and off-balance.

"Lok Yui noticed the head of a 'seasoned-looking man' as it came into view. The man had close-cropped hair, a steady gaze, and looked very strong. Standing directly behind Locust Eater, he appeared to be controlling both of his arms.

"Arms flying in the wild abandon of pursuit, Cheng Bok and Ah Tu drew to a halt. There, right there, panting on the ground was Lok Yiu. They had him at last. But what was Locust Eater doing there, and who was the strange old man holding him so firmly? Cheng Bok decided to challenge the old man. 'Hey old man, what do you think you are up to?' he said. 'Get on home, before you get into something you'll regret.'

"Mah Tsu merely smiled, inclining his head to one side as he did so.

"Ah Tu decided to follow Cheng Bok's example. 'Get lost grey-head, or we'll . . .'

"The roar seemed to be a long way off, until Ah Tu realized that it was right next to him. Galvanized into action, he lunged at the old

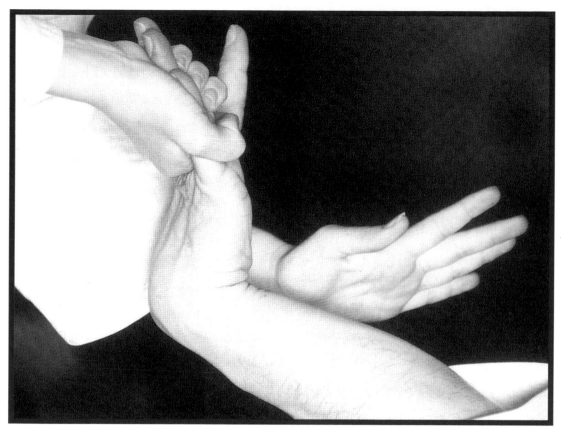

**One of the keys to the effective practice of jujutsu is found in the following principle: Control the wrist joint and you can control the elbow, the shoulder, the back, and ultimately the whole body.**

man, who had emitted the spirit shout. Within the same instant, he was thrown high up into the air so that there was a great deal of space between his body and the ground. Without training in the martial arts, his thin frame hit the ground so hard that the wind was knocked out of him, and he was left gasping for air.

"Mah Tsu reluctantly released his grip on the cowardly Locust Eater to deal with Cheng Bok, who attacked next. The attack was so feeble, uncoordinated, and amateurish, that Mah Tsu regretted loosing his grip on Locust Eater, who was now trying in vain to flee. A man with a smashed right leg had hold of him and was clinging on to him with all his might.

"Running to the scene from way behind, Chu was baffled. Thick clouds of dust billowed up, and a mêlée of bodies moved oddly in the commotion. He saw one man clinging to the 'fox' of a waiter they had caught in the gambling hall...The man clinging to the waiter was almost dragged along, and he saw another man, fighting painfully for breath. Old Mah Tsu was holding a struggling man. What was going on, and where had all these men come from?

" 'Keep still everyone, or someone will get hurt,' the old man said with quiet authority. Strangely, they complied. One by one, Mah Tsu removed the sashes from the struggling men's pants and neatly bound their hands."

## SINGLE-HAND ESCAPE AND COUNTER

Your opponent grabs your hand (let us assume palm-up). Using your free hand, reach under your opponent's free hand and grab around the base of his or her thumb as you step to your left (your opponent's right). Rotate, and twist your opponent's hand counterclockwise. This will cause your opponent to go to the ground. This technique is an example of jujutsu applied "passively" (in that you are grabbed and simply respond rather than attack).

## FOUR-FINGER CONTROL

In the technique just described, the defender was passive. In this technique, however, the defender is active: as the defender, you initiate the action. Grab the fingers of your opponent's right hand using

## SINGLE-HAND ESCAPE AND COUNTER

**STEP 1:** Seize your partner's wrist and place your palms on the back of his or her hand and grip it.

**STEP 2:** Twist in a counterclockwise direction to effect the technique.

your left hand. Push your opponent's hand downward, and bend the fingers upward. This will tighten, and finally lock, your opponent's tendons. Now pivot 90 degrees clockwise, and turn your opponent's hand clockwise. Grab the back of your opponent's right elbow using your right hand, and step up close to him or her. Both of you should now

## FOUR-FINGER CONTROL

Bending your partner's fingers up and back, and keeping his elbow straight, "lift" him or her to effect the technique.

be facing the same direction. As you perform the stepping-up action, lift your opponent's fingers directly upward, and keep his or her elbow locked.

## WRIST AND ELBOW LOCKS

The effective application of wrist and elbow locks relies on two basic categories of movement. In the first category, a wrist is twisted clockwise or counterclockwise, and the elbow is twisted into the center until it cannot go any farther. In the second category, the elbow is twisted and locked out, so it cannot bend.

These two basic categories of movements are divided into two types of grips and two types of grip reversals (a grip reversal is when you have been gripped, whereupon you turn the tables on your opponent and grip him or her). The efficiency of both categories is improved if you step to the side of your opponent's body as you apply a technique.

## GRIP A

Grip your opponent's right wrist as shown, and stretch your opponent to the side. Place your right arm horizontally, making sure that the elbow of your gripping hand is slightly higher than your wrist. You could, for added efficiency, grasp your opponent's fingers with your free left hand and support the lock by further twisting them (not shown).

## GRIP B

**STEP 1:** Catch your opponent's wrist with your left hand, gripping the little finger edge of the hand. Twist your opponent's forearm bones to their maximum position, as shown.

**STEP 2:** Follow through with the gripping hand to bring your opponent to the ground. You may use your free hand to support the lock by pressing on your opponent's elbow to ensure it is straightened and that he or she is immobilized.

Jujutsu employs dangerous groundwork techniques, and some of the strangles and chokes are effective enough to cause death. Some schools have therefore eliminated them from the syllabus, while others practice them under the strictest supervision.

## GROUNDWORK HOLDS

**Groundwork** holds, as the term implies, deal with the art of restraining an opponent on the ground. Opinions vary among jujutsu teachers as to the original purpose of groundwork holds. Some believe they were developed with an emphasis on utterly disabling—or even killing—an opponent in a life-and-death situation. Others believe original jujutsu followed in the tradition of civil-arrest techniques, and thus, the purpose of a groundwork hold is to control an opponent to the point of submission.

It is the author's opinion that because of jujutsu's close association with the resuscitation arts, such as kappo or katsu, (for example, reviving

It is vital to have medical assistance present during any kind of competition or tournament, as occasionally injury rears its ugly head. This injured competitor is placed in the recovery position.

people who have been rendered unconscious in a groundwork choking technique), it is reasonable to assume the purpose of groundwork probably lies in subduing an opponent. If this were to be done with too much enthusiasm, however, at least the practitioner would be in a position to revive the stricken opponent.

Groundwork holds are generally divided into three classes of techniques: choking techniques (shime-waza), pinning techniques (osaekomi-waza), and joint-locking techniques on the ground (kansetsu-waza). All are normally applied after a throw, trip, or submission, but they can be applied no matter how the opponent gets to the ground.

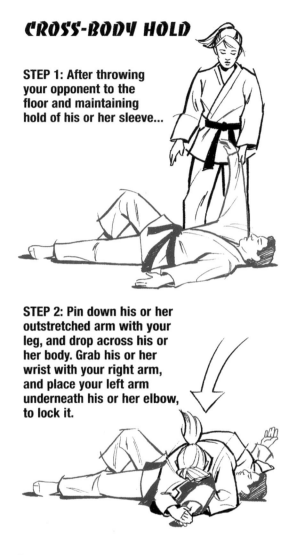

## CROSS-BODY HOLD

**STEP 1:** After throwing your opponent to the floor and maintaining hold of his or her sleeve...

**STEP 2:** Pin down his or her outstretched arm with your leg, and drop across his or her body. Grab his or her wrist with your right arm, and place your left arm underneath his or her elbow, to lock it.

## CROSS-BODY HOLD

With your opponent on the ground, keep hold of his or her right sleeve with your left hand. Step over the seized arm, drop to both your knees, and trap his or her left arm between your legs. Let go with your left hand, and lie across your opponent's chest, pinning him or her to the floor. Grab his

# JUJUTSU

## COMBINATION TECHNIQUE

**STEP 1:** Entangle your opponent's right arm and bend it.

**STEP 2:** Swing him or her to the ground. Try to prevent him or her from banging his or her head.

**STEP 3:** Keep your fallen opponent immobilized as shown.

**STEP 4:** Another variation you could use is to straighten your opponent's arm and lock the elbow using your knee.

or her left wrist with your right hand. Stretching out, pin your opponent's arm to the floor while stretching your left arm under his or her elbow in a figure-four shape. You will have achieved a strong position of leverage under your opponent's elbow. Take care, however, as it can break an opponent's elbow joint.

## COMBINATION TECHNIQUES

Combination techniques require you to combine, in a smooth, orderly sequence, a series of individual techniques. The following technique is a combination of striking, wrist and elbow locking, throwing, and groundwork holding.

Your opponent attacks you with a straight right punch to your face. Keeping covered, slide to the right side of the attack, and block the punch with the edges of your forearms. Grab the attacker's right wrist with your right hand, and push, slap, or strike your opponent's face. Bring your left hand over and under your opponent's right arm to entangle it. Pivoting 180 degrees counterclockwise, press your opponent's bent, trapped wrist and elbow joints downward, throwing him or her to the ground. Be sure to keep your back straight and your head up as you bend your knees and follow your falling opponent to the ground, sitting as closely as possible on arrival. Bring both knees close to your opponent's head, and maintain the wristlock.

## STRANGLE LOCK (HADAKAJIME)

The strangle lock is applied without making use of your opponent's clothing. There are several variations of this lock, but it is generally applied from behind your opponent. Resting on your left knee, pass your

The sliding lapel strangle, although undoubtedly effective, is best applied by someone with considerable physical strength over his or her opponent. The victim can still thrash wildly, because his or her back is still relatively straight.

right arm around your opponent's throat from behind, and then bring it back over his or her left shoulder until you can grab your own left upper arm. Press the back of your opponent's head with your left arm. By combining a pulling motion with your right hand with a forward pressure from your left hand against the back of your opponent's head, you can effect the strangle lock.

## SLIDING LAPEL STRANGLE (OKURIERI)

This strangle hold is applied from behind your sitting opponent. Pass your right arm over his or her right shoulder and grasp his or her left collar. Now pass your left arm under your opponent's left armpit until it can grip the right front of your opponent's collar. Bringing your hands closer to his or her throat, pull him or her backward until the choke is effective; that is, until it causes the opponent to submit.

In recent years, the supremacy of strangulation techniques has been proven in many incidences of real-life, no-holds-barred combat. These combats often take place as Mixed Martial Arts (MMA) events. Some jujutsu teachers consider these fights to be brutal and unworthy spectacles, while others see them as opportunities to test techniques.

**WORDS TO UNDERSTAND**

**jojutsu** Techniques for using a Japanese staff

**tai-waza** Body technique

**Zen** Meditation and a type of Buddhism

# Throwing Techniques and Weapons

**Throwing techniques, known as nage, are at the heart of both judo and jujutsu. The basic idea behind throwing techniques is that the more forceful the opponent's attack, the more forcefully he or she will be thrown.**

Throws are useful if, for example, you are charged or crowded by an opponent. Indeed, if such an opponent should end up flat on his or her back as a result of a throw, the jujutsu practitioner can rightly enjoy a sense of "fair play." Generally speaking, throws are conducted at extremely close range, and are usually referred to as "body techniques" (or **tai-waza**). This label distinguishes them from all other techniques. It is possible to move from a joint-locking technique (or any other technique) to a throwing technique.

Throwing techniques are best classified according to the methods that are used to achieve them. For example, you could trip and throw an opponent by placing your leg behind him or her as an obstacle, and then cause him or her to fall down by pushing him or her over your leg.

**Down, but not out. This spectacular dropping throw, would, in all probability, be followed up with a groundwork technique, except during a tournament, in which it would have scored a full point, or ippon.**

Another throwing method is to literally turn your back on your opponent and then pull him or her around your hip and leg. A third method—possibly the most dramatic of these examples—involves placing your back and shoulder up and under an opponent and then throwing him or her over your shoulder.

## LEG-REAPING THROW (OSOTO GARI)

Judo and jujutsu both practice the leg-reaping throw (known as os oto gari). To perform this throw, grasp the sleeve and collar of your

**Making break-falls is sometimes referred to as ukemi, particularly in aikido ("spirit harmony way"), which is derived from jujutsu.**

opponent's clothing, and then raise your right leg. Now push your hip toward your opponent's hip, with the goal of placing your right leg tightly behind your opponent's right leg. Make sure you keep the knee of your supporting leg well bent to maintain your balance. Try to move smoothly, so as not to indicate your intentions. Now, hook your right leg backward in a strong, reaping motion, then bend forward at the waist and throw your opponent backward onto the ground.

## HIP THROW (OGOSHI)

The hip throw (known as ogoshi) is another throw that jujutsu shares with judo. To perform the hip throw, grasp your opponent's sleeve and collar. Step in toward his or her right foot, while dropping your right arm around your opponent's back. Now pull your opponent's right arm up and forward.

## LEG-REAPING THROW

**STEP 1: Keeping your back straight and your knees bent, close with your partner.**

**STEP 2: Swiftly hook/catch his or her leg with yours and break his or her posture by bending his or her back.**

**STEP 3: Effect the throw by swinging him or her around his or her own entangled leg.**

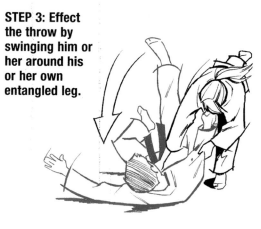

## JUJUTSU

The idea is to bring your opponent's weight onto his or her right leg. You must pivot counterclockwise, so that you face the same direction as your opponent. Bending your knees, so that your pelvis is lower than that of your opponent, extend your right hip beyond your opponent's right hip, and continue to draw his or her right arm forward. Lever your opponent onto your right hip, then smoothly straighten both legs while bending forward at the waist. This movement should flip your opponent over and onto his or her back.

## HIP THROW

STEP 1: Turn your hip in toward your opponent's waist.

STEP 2: Swing your opponent over and around your hip.

## SHOULDER THROW

**STEP 1:** Push sideways into your opponent's shoulder, placing it as closely as possible, near or under his or her arm.

**STEP 2:** Continue to pivot/turn and literally throw your opponent over your shoulder.

# SHOULDER THROW (SEOI NAGE)

To perform the shoulder throw, grasp your opponent's sleeve and collar. Now pull your opponent's right arm forward and upward. Step forward on your right foot and, pivoting counterclockwise, continue to pull on your opponent's arm, locking it as close to your shoulder as possible. Make sure that your right shoulder fits neatly into your opponent's right armpit (you will need to bend your knees to do this). At this point, you should be facing in the same direction as your opponent. Pull him or her forward against your back to take him or her off-balance. Finish the throw by bending sharply at the waist and lifting your opponent off your back and onto the ground. Stay in a strong, upright position when the throw has been completed, and do not let go of your opponent's arm (keeping control of the arm will allow you to apply a follow-up technique).

## JUJUTSU AND WEAPONS

As an art of self-defense, jujutsu involves defending against a variety of weapons. Some jujutsu schools introduce this concept right at the start of training; other schools believe that training against weapons should begin only after a degree of competence in defending against unarmed attacks is reached. Irrespective of either view, the stark fact is that defending against a weapon is a tricky business.

In jujutsu training, students sometimes wield weapons so that fellow students can how learn to defend against them. You may also be taught the skills and coordination necessary to wield a weapon for the sheer enjoyment of it. A jujutsu practitioner with only a few months' training who thinks that he or she can face an armed thug or gang of thugs is probably seriously misguided. Real life is not like the movies, in which the bad guys never seem to be able to shoot straight. Training to defend against weapon attacks in jujutsu takes time. This type of training should best be viewed as a confidence-builder.

Traditional jujutsu uses a collection of Japanese weapons. These include a short stick known as a yawara, a short wooden knife known as a tanto, a short wooden sword known as a wakisashi, a full-length sword known as a bokken, and Japanese short and long staffs known as the jo and bo, respectively. Wooden weapons are relatively inexpensive compared with their traditional steel counterparts. Moreover, they are safer to train with and require no maintenance.

Other traditional weapons include a weighted chain called a

manriki- guari, which was used to capture other weapons, and an iron fan called a tessan, which was carried by many samurai warriors. High-ranking samurai, right up to the emperor himself, would not allow weapons to be carried in their presence. However, the iron fan was an exception to this rule, as it could provide a degree of defense against an edged weapon, should treachery occur. The iron war fan could be used to deflect blows, render a counterattack, or obscure an enemy's vision.

Modern jujutsu training seeks to counter a less traditional and more eclectic array of weapons, including cut-up plastic bottles (to simulate broken glass bottles); rubber daggers; pick-ax handles; pieces of timber, cardboard, and plastic tubing; and even fake guns. The following outlines a few methods for using the jo, to give you a feeling for weapon usage in jujutsu. You are, however, strongly advised not to undertake any weapons training without competent instruction and supervision.

## THE JO

Strictly speaking, the jo is not exclusively a jujutsu weapon. Other types of martial arts, including aikido and karate, use the jo as well. The

## ATTACKERS' WITH GUNS

To say that there is an effective defense against an attacker with a gun is problematic at best and foolish at worst (although it is not foolish if there is no alternative). A trigger can be squeezed quickly. Also, a sudden rush to try and disarm someone armed with a gun could cause him or her to panic and fire—the last outcome you want.

jo combines the techniques of the Japanese halberd (called the naginata), the spear, and even the sword. Despite its apparent simplicity, the jo is a weapon capable of being used with the greatest of skill and subtlety.

Indeed, the story of its development in 17th-century Japan is a great source of inspiration to anyone interested in learning about an ancient, yet simple and inexpensive weapon.

In the early 15th century, Japan's greatest swordsman, Musashi Miyamoto, fell into a duel with a martial arts master named Muso Gonnosuke, whom he soundly defeated. Musashi, a formidable swordsman, had developed a style of swordsmanship that used two swords simultaneously. Most samurai carried two swords and a dagger, and the two-sword combination worn at the sash was called the daisho. Gonnosuke had fought Musashi using a six-foot (1.8-m) pole called a bow. Musashi, however, had caught the bow in a cross-sword combination, which made it impossible for Gonnosuke to retrieve his weapon. Fortunately, Musashi spared Gonnosuke's life.

Shamed and dispirited, Gonnosuke retreated to a mountain in isolation, to spend time reflecting upon his defeat. He appears to have arrived at the idea that the bow, which was six feet (1.8 m) in length, lacked maneuverability, particularly at middle and close ranges. This insight led him to develop techniques suitable for a shorter, four-foot staff, and thus the jo was invented. He called the style of fighting using a jo shindo muso ryu jojutsu. Gonnosuke fought a second duel with Musashi, and incredibly, was the only man ever to defeat him.

The jo is usually made of red Japanese oak or a similar hard wood. It is approximately 50 inches (127 cm) in length and almost an inch (2.5 cm) in diameter. A sword cannot cut through a one-inch-thick oak jo. The length

**The samurai hero, Yashitzone, in combat with an armored opponent in an engraving by Emil Barraud.**

of the jo allows for versatility in usage, especially in changes of grip; in swinging and turning the weapon; and in being able to strike using both ends of the weapon.

Because the technique of using the jo (called **jojutsu**) was developed for use against a sword, sword techniques are common in its repertoire. However, unlike the sword, the jo also acts as a "pole arm," and includes the receiving actions, entering motions, and thrusts of classic spear and halberd techniques.

# GRIPPING THE JO

To use the jo effectively, you need to learn how to transfer the full force and power of your body into the weapon and, ultimately, into the target. If your grip on the jo is poor, your technique will fail. The proper grip for a jo is similar to that of a sword.

The jo is best gripped using the strongest parts of the hand, which are the last three fingers of the hand and the thumb. The index finger is not used when gripping the jo because it will interfere with the strongest natural gripping position. A good Japanese swordsperson will "float" the index finger of both hands when using a sword, as does the user of a jo. This practice is not confined to weapon usage alone; in a traditional training fist for karate gripping that has been passed down

## GRIPPING THE JO

A firm but flexible and changeable grip is essential. Without it, it is impossible to swing the jo and change the direction it is traveling in.

through the centuries, the index finger is excluded.

Sometimes, a particular jo technique requires the grip to be relaxed, in which case the thumb and index finger may hold the staff, but this would seldom be at the point of contact with an opponent. To grip the jo properly, squeeze the jo with the last three fingers of each hand, while keeping your thumbs and index fingers rolled into the jo.

## BASIC STANCES FOR USING THE JO

There are two basic stances for using a jo. For the first one, called the sankakutai posture, stand in a left-leg-forward, T-shaped stance, with your left foot pointing toward your opponent. Your right foot should be turned out a minimum of 60 degrees and a maximum of 90 degrees to the right. Your feet should be no more than shoulder-width apart. Stand in a relaxed manner, with your knees bent and your center of gravity fixed equally between your feet. Your shoulders and hips should face approximately 45 degrees to the right (this half-facing posture is referred to as hanmi); this posture helps you present less of a target to your opponent. Your right arm should be relaxed at your side, while your left hand should hold the jo vertically.

For the second stance, called chudan no kamae, stand as in the sankakutai posture, grip the jo with both hands, and hold it out at middle level. This is a traditional sword posture; it is also used in kendo ("the way of the sword") and iaido ("the art of drawing, cutting with, and replacing the sword").

There is also a more threatening posture in which the jo is held above the head, ready to strike.

## BASIC STANCES

**BASIC UPRIGHT STANCE:** Your body is held relaxed but ready, and the jo is held perpendicular and away from the body.

**BASIC READY STANCE:** This is similar to the basic posture or "attitude" used in Japanese fencing.

# BASIC TECHNIQUES USING THE JO

There are four basic techniques for which the jo is used: thrusting, striking, sweeping, and receiving. A thrust is the action of spearing the end of a jo toward and into the target. There are three basic types of thrust: the underhand thrust, in which the forward hand is palm-up and the rear hand palm-down; the overhand thrust, in which both hands are palm-down; and the reverse-hand thrust, in which the jo is held at face level, with the forward hand facing away from you and the back hand facing toward you.

There are many ways of striking with a jo, but the most basic strike involves three separate actions. In the first action, you swing your arms downward—particularly the bottom hand, which provides most of the power for the strike. In the second action, you twist your hands. This action puts the force of your wrists into the strike as well, and ensures that your grip can withstand the impact of the strike. In the third action, carried out just before impact, the jo is flexed and extended.

## JUJUTSU AND ZEN

**Zen** is a Japanese word used to describe a system of meditation linked with a spiritual lifestyle. Zen thinking and practice has underpinned a considerable amount of Japanese culture. It has influenced everything from swordsmanship to the making of a cup of tea. In fact, the famous "tea ceremony" can still be observed today in Japan. Japanese martial arts received a profound input from Zen Buddhism during the 16th century.

Zen meditation is designed to inquire into the true nature of things and to become wise and, ultimately, enlightened. Martial artists have used meditation for centuries to calm the mind, instill mental discipline, and to provide a broader

### BASIC THRUST

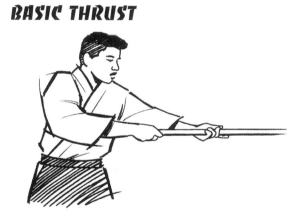

STEP 1: From the basic position, prepare to lunge forward...

STEP 2: After lunging your body forward, thrust the jo towards your intended target, taking care not to overcommit yourself.

## BASIC STRIKING

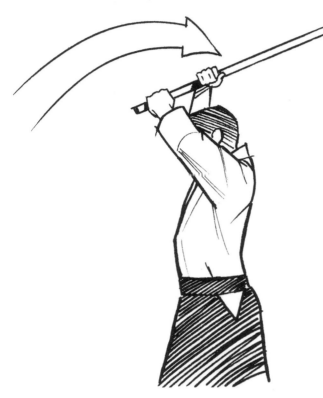

**Raise the jo above your head with a strong feeling and prepare to swing down in a powerful cutting action.**

life view than was commonly experienced by professional soldiers or warriors.

Zen meditation is best done alone in a quiet place. You can meditate for as short a time as two minutes to as long a time as you like. To practice Zen meditation, sit either cross-legged on the floor or on a straight-backed chair. Keeping your back straight, swell out your abdomen and put a little strength there, then relax. Close your mouth, and leave your eyes slightly open. Breathe through your nose, and become very still. Empty your mind, clearing away distractions like fear, anger, or greed. Try to set aside all thoughts, emotions, ideas, and beliefs—even the sense of who you are.

This is how those who meditate achieve a state referred to as "empty." In the state of "empty," you can gain "the way," find "the center" of both yourself and the universe, and sit fearlessly within. This "still center" is a place of great balance and power. It is peaceful, but dynamic; tranquil, but eventful; instant, yet eternal.

## JOJUTSU TARGETS

The targets used in jojutsu are the same as those used in jujutsu: the vital points (atemi-waza). Strikes at these targets can produce pain, temporary paralysis, unconsciousness, or even death. The result depends on the target, the amount of force used, and the physical condition of the person struck. Common jojutsu targets are:

- The point of the forehead (tento)—downward strikes.
- The temples (kasumi)—side strikes.
- The point between the eyes (uto)—thrusts or high jabs.
- The throat (sonu)—thrusts or high jabs.
- The solar plexus (suigetsu)—thrusts.
- The elbows (hiji)—usually attacked when the opponent's arms are raised. Sweeps directed from underneath the elbows are effective.
- The wrists (tekubi)—most effectively attacked using high sweeps or strikes when the opponent's arms are raised, or with strikes when the opponent's arms are lowered.
- The backs of the hands (hokashiyakuzawa)—high sweeps if the opponent's hands are raised, strikes if they are lowered.
- The testicles (kinsho)—a common target in cruder forms of jujutsu; less common for the jo.
- The knees (hiza)—sweeps, occasionally kneeling strikes.
- The ankles (kurabushi)—sweeps.
- The tops of the feet (kori)—thrusts or jabs.

## FREEDOM FROM FEAR

This section is provided to illustrate the true (practical) value of the Zen mind to the martial artist.

As plants spring forth from seeds, so thoughts spring forth from minds. It is the ability to let go of these thoughts and cease to identify with them that truly liberates. In the book *Buddhist Scriptures*, selected and translated by Edward Conze, we read:

"For whatever a man thinks about continually, to that his mind becomes inclined by the force of habit; for unwholesome thoughts will grow when nursed in the heart and breed misfortune for yourself and others alike."

According to Zen Buddhism:

"Physical discomfort and suffering are not the same thing. We suffer in the mind, and the mind produces the conditions of life, which are

**Contemplation and concentration are two of the hallmarks of Oriental martial arts, like jujutsu, as we have seen in this book, and are undoubtedly influenced by Zen Buddhism.**

unstable and unsatisfactory.

"If, by renouncing a lesser happiness one attains to a happiness that is greater, then let the wise pursue that happiness, which is greater." — Dhammapada: 290

Harmonizing with an attack and effortlessly defeating it gives perhaps one of the greatest modern insights into Zen.

## AFTERWORD

"The willow tree bends, we are told. The willow tree does not bend itself, however. It is bent by the force of the wind and springs back as a result of that force. So do we train our bodies and minds, by aspiring to be like a perfect mirror for force. Not by judging, condemning, or punishing, but by rising above our own prejudice, bias, or fear. When we practice jujutsu, we should be neither aggressive nor passive. We should simply seek to absorb, neutralize, and return an opponent's force. Thus, an opponent's attack should lead to his or her defeat."

Finally, bear in mind that jujutsu may contribute to your physical and mental abilities, but do not dwell in your imagination on scenes of conflict and confrontation with which to punish or frighten yourself or others.

"He who is streetwise may be hailed a success as a fighter, but his credentials as a human being may be found severely wanting. The ultimate opponent is yourself, the greatest impediment to your own success."

I hope you have enjoyed this introduction to jujutsu. The subject is inexhaustible, and I have only been able to introduce the bones of it. Only competent training can add muscle, sinew, and flesh. Good luck training!

# GLOSSARY

| | |
|---|---|
| **Aikido** | "The way of harmony"; a modern Japanese martial art |
| **Atemi-waza** | Nerve-point or pressure-point strikes used in martial arts |
| **Chudan** | Middle level |
| **Dan** | Levels of black belt |
| **Dojo** | A martial arts training hall |
| **Feudal** | Social and political system in which peasants work for a powerful landowner in exchange for food and protection |
| **Gedan** | Lower level |
| **Groundwork** | Actions performed when both fighters are on the ground |
| **Halberd** | A battle-ax and pike mounted on a long handle |
| **Jodan** | Upper level |
| **Jojutsu** | Techniques for using a Japanese staff |
| **Kenpo** | General Japanese term for fist art |
| **Kyu** | A series of grades or ranks below black belt |
| **Layperson** | A regular worshiper, as opposed to a monk or nun |
| **Nanushi** | Agents of brothel keepers during the Edo period in Japan (1603-1867) |
| **Peripheral vision** | The 180-degree vision possible when the eyes are unfocused |

| | |
|---|---|
| **Rei** | Formal traditional bow |
| **Resuscitation** | Reviving an unconscious person |
| **Sensei** | The traditional name given to martial arts teachers |
| **Shihonzuki** | Four-finger strike |
| **Ukemi** | Japanese general term for breaking a fall |
| **Tai-waza** | Body technique |
| **Yawara-ge** | "Peace-making"; fighting without weapons |
| **Yojori-kumi-uchi** | Samurai grappling |
| **Yoshin-ryu** | "The willow-heart school"; an early version of jujutsu |
| **Zen** | Meditation and a type of Buddhism |

# CLOTHING

**Gi**: The gi is the most typical martial arts "uniform." Usually in white, but also available in other colors, it consists of a cotton thigh-length jacket and calf-length trousers. Gis come in three weights: light, medium, and heavy. Lightweight gis are cooler than heavyweight gis, but not as strong. The jacket is usually bound at the waist with a belt.

**Belt**: Belts are used in the martial arts to denote the rank and experience of the wearer. They are made from strong linen or cotton and wrap several times around the body before tying. Beginners usually wear a white belt, and the final belt is almost always black.

**Hakama**: A long folded skirt with five pleats at the front and one at the back. It is a traditional form of clothing in kendo, iaido, and jujutsu.

**Zori:** A simple pair of slip-on sandals worn in the dojo when not training to keep the floor clean.

# WEAPONS

**Bokken**: A bokken is a long wooden sword made from Japanese oak. Bokken are roughly the same size and shape as a traditional Japanese sword (katana).

**Jo:** The jo is a simple wooden staff about 4–5 ft (1.3 – 1.6 m) long and is a traditional weapon of karate and aikido.

**Kamma:** Two short-handled sickles used as a fighting tool in some types of karate and jujutsu.

**Tanto:** A wooden knife used for training purposes.

**Hojo jutsu:** A long rope with a noose on one end used in jujutsu to restrain attackers.

**Sai**: Long, thin, and sharp spikes, held like knives and featuring wide, spiked handguards just above the handles.

**Tonfa:** Short poles featuring side handles, like modern-day police batons.

**Katana:** A traditional Japanese sword with a slightly curved blade and a single, razor-sharp cutting edge.

**Butterfly knives:** A pair of knives, each one with a wide blade. They are used mainly in kung fu.

**Nunchaku:** A flail-like weapon consisting of three short sections of staff connected by chains.

**Shinai:** A bamboo training sword used in the martial art of kendo.

**Iaito:** A stainless-steel training sword with a blunt blade used in the sword-based martial art of iaido.

## TRAINING AIDS

**Mook yan jong**: A wooden dummy against which the martial artist practices his blocks and punches and conditions his limbs for combat.

**Makiwara**: A plank of wood set in the ground used for punching and kicking practice.

**Focus pads**: Circular pads worn on the hands by one person, while his or her partner uses the pads for training accurate punching.

## PROTECTIVE EQUIPMENT

**Headguard**: A padded, protective helmet that protects the wearer from blows to the face and head.

**Joint supports**: Tight foam or bandage sleeves that go around elbow, knee, or ankle joints and protect the muscles and joints against damage during training.

**Groin protector**: A well-padded undergarment for men that protects the testicles and the abdomen from kicks and low punches.

**Practice mitts**: Lightweight boxing gloves that protect the wearer's hands from damage in sparring, and reduce the risk of cuts being inflicted on the opponent.

**Chest protector**: A sturdy shield worn by women over the chest to protect the breasts during sparring.

# FURTHER READING

Gagne, Tammy. *Trends in Martial Arts.* Hockessin, Delaware: Mitchell Lane Publishers, 2014.

Reilly, Robin L. *Karate for Kids.* North Clarendon, Vermont: Charles E. Tuttle Co, 2012
Note: This is part of a series from the publisher that breaks down the martial arts by discipline. Similar titles are available for taekwondo, judo, and others.

Stone, Jeff. *The Five Ancestors (Series).* New York: Random House Books for Young Readers, 2009.
Note: A series of novels tracks the adventures of a family of young martial artists in 17th-century China.

# SERIES CONSULTANT

**Adam James** is the Founder of Rainbow Warrior Martial Arts and the Director for the National College of Exercise Professionals. Adam is a 10th Level Instructor of Wei Kuen Do, Chi Fung, and Modern Escrima, and a 5th Degree Black Belt in Kempo, Karate, Juijitsu, and Kobudo. He is also the co-creator of the NCEP-Rainbow Warrior Martial Arts MMA Trainer certification program, which has been endorsed by the Commissioner of MMA for the State of Hawaii and by the U.S. Veterans Administration. Adam was also the Director of World Black Belt, whose Founding Members include Chuck Norris, Bob Wall, Gene LeBell, and 50 of the world's greatest martial artists. In addition, Adam is an actor, writer and filmmaker, and he has performed with Andy Garcia, Tommy Lee Jones, and Steven Seagal. As a writer, he has been published in numerous martial arts books and magazines, including *Black Belt, Masters Magazine*, and the *Journal of Asian Martial Arts*, and he has written several feature film screenplays.

# Useful Web Sites

http//martialarts.org/
A general guide to various martial arts.

http://www.danzan.com/
This site is run by Prof. Henry Seishiro Okazaki, a teacher and jujutsu historian.

http://www.usjjf.org/home.htm
Site of the U.S. Jiu-Jitsu Federation, which organizes competitions in jiujitsu and jujutsu.

**Publisher's Note:** The websites listed on this page were active at the time of publication. The publisher is not responsible for websites that have changed their address or discontinued operation since the date of publication. The publisher reviews and updates the websites each time the book is reprinted.

# About the Author

**Nathan Johnson** holds a 6th-dan black belt in karate and a 4th-degree black sash in traditional Chinese kung fu. He has studied martial arts for 30 years and holds seminars and lectures on martial arts and related subjects throughout the world. He teaches zen shorindo karate at several leading universities in the U.K. His previous books include *Zen Shaolin Karate* and *Barefoot Zen*. He lives in Hampshire, England.

# NDEX